The Crane

T0338894

The Waste

The Dump

The Asbestos

The Coal

The Smoke

The Plants

The Home

The Trucks

The Cargo

The High-Speed Rail

The Flights

The Institutions

The Vacancies

The Entrance

The Sign

The Partnership

The Figures

The Plaza

The Land

The Fences

The Register

The Thresholds

The Shade

The Music

The Water

The Streets

The Occupants

The Paintings

The Landmark

The Cashmere

The Goats

The Sitters

The Noise

The Residents

The Landscape

The Birds

The Neighbourhood

The Construction

The Public

The Private

The Edge

The Things Around Us

51N4E
Rural Urban Framework

Canadian Centre for Architecture
jovis

The Offices

FROM WITHIN AN ECOLOGY OF PRACTICE
Francesco Garutti

The potential for architects to be influential and transformative agents of space has been increasingly contested by the developmental logic of neoliberal urbanism. Often called upon to simply participate in, rather than shape, transformation processes, twenty-first-century architects are confined by the rules of an uncompromising market and its restrictive, conformist design ideologies, employing practice only as a "decorative tool."[1] With the possibility of a radical reframing of space now hampered, many architects today find themselves reduced to service providers, asked only to improve the marketability of developers' projects with surface-level features like well-being and sustainability. Given these conditions, the need to reconsider the character and scope of the architect's role grows ever more pressing.

More than simply the practice of building itself, with aesthetic and programmatic parameters taking the lead in informing design work, the process of making architecture today is moulded by an overwhelming coagulation of economic, social, and political forces. The debate in the discipline between contextualism—the idea that buildings should be derived from their context, physical, temporal, or cultural—and autonomy—according to which architecture is an independent aesthetic product—is therefore increasingly irrelevant. Context means something wholly different in today's polymorphous, extensive, and global urban space. To reassess what architects can do, we need to examine the frameworks within which they operate, redefining the concept of context and questioning its use. An updated vocabulary and a new catalogue of tools to analyze global urbanization processes are perhaps good places to start.[2] But we also need to recognize and learn from those architects applying these new ideas of context both in and on space.

51N4E and Rural Urban Framework (RUF), two offices active in what seem distant and distinct geographical areas—the centre of post-

1   See Teddy Cruz, "Rethinking Urban Growth: It's About Inequality, Stupid," in *Uneven Growth: Tactical Urbanism for Expanding Megacities*, ed. Pedro Gadanho (New York: Museum of Modern Art, 2014), 51.

2   Christian Schmid et al., "Towards a New Vocabulary of Urbanisation Processes: A Comparative Approach," *Urban Studies* 55, no. 1 (January 2018): 19–52.

The Generic

socialist Tirana, the neglected corners of twenty-first-century Brussels, a string of rural Chinese villages, and the fringe of settlement in Ulaanbaatar—offer insightful case studies on the role of the architect within the dynamics of planetary urbanization. Attuned to the political and economic forces tied into every project and every site, both offices superimpose large and small scales in their work, rethinking site-specificity along entirely new lines. Together, they complexify the very notion of context in architecture, seeing it as alive, metabolic, and conversational, and moreover, defined by an interwoven network of manifold systems and influences. Context, 51N4E's and RUF's work suggests, overwhelms us into abandoning our posts. And in this expanded definition, it forces us to rethink what it means to practice architecture.

In different ways and at different speeds, 51N4E and RUF formed and evolved as living, collective organisms, each absorbing and exploring a range of territories over the years and continually hybridizing research and design. For both, the metamorphosis of their practices began as a physical journey, a process of shifting vantage or of reading the landscape. In 2004, Freek Persyn and Johan Anrys of 51N4E took their first trip to Tirana, marking both the beginning of a decade of research and design work in Albania and the launch of an integrated, on-site laboratory. Likewise, in 2005, John Lin and Joshua Bolchover of RUF travelled from Hong Kong to a project site through the provinces of Guangdong and Guanxi, sparking their first study of the composite, transitional territories linking the urban and rural in southern China. The journey, for 51N4E and RUF, is not simply a worn-out metaphor for a cognitive experience; it is a physical state in which frictions and overlaps between geopolitical forces, legislative anomalies, environmental situations, and economic and social contradictions redefine every assumption about how to practice architecture. For both offices, the journey is an act of careful observation and of listening, an attempt to understand and to adopt and adapt practical and ideological tools. It is an approach that absorbs and incorporates different methodologies according to changing constraints, and one that listens for new voices.

Back in 2006, when architects and researchers in China were still focused on the study and development of the megalopolis, Lin and Bolchover began to explore the processes of urbanization from

The Sky

another perspective. Crossing the Chinese countryside to study hybrid city-countryside geographies and forms of settlement, they identified the terrain of their work in the contradictions of the accepted rural-urban dichotomy. This gave rise to RUF as an independent laboratory embedded in the University of Hong Kong. Lin and Bolchover delimited their field to places where small-scale instances of architecture and the built environment testify, as evidence, to large-scale policy shift and social change.

Around the same time, 51N4E won a significant competition for the construction of a tower building in the heart of Tirana. Caught between worldviews and population shifts, between its historical isolation and its recent openness to the global market, Tirana was the heart of what was then the youngest post-socialist democracy in Europe, yearning for ideas and desires that could redefine its political and social identity. The competition and the TID Tower 51N4E designed in response gave rise to an extended landscape of new projects and research in Albania, launching a twelve-year chapter in the office's history that would go on to transform its methodologies. Working with the uncertainty of political reconstruction, a new class of leaders, and a precarious, fragile economy, the office underwent a conceptual and structural metamorphosis during its time in Albania that the architects brought back with them to Brussels. Tirana was a testing ground, where the very heart of the design process shifted to absorb unpredictability, dialogue, and friction, and where empathy, engagement with local communities, and a mutual sense of trust between players were the most necessary ingredients.

Both offices, through different strategies and learning from distant geographical contexts, absorb and incorporate a wealth of actors, alliances, and collaborations that expand the architects' ecological system, significantly redefining their tools and position. The building itself, in this new ecology of practice, is now more than ever just one piece of an extended system—the final outcome of a long sequence of actions undertaken in the transformation of a territory by a web of agents. But it is also a mechanism designed to resolve—or rather, to reveal—the conflicts, anomalies, and contradictions intrinsic to a new, expanded definition of context. Decomposed, dissected, and reassembled, context—the people, tools, policies, economies, times, and scales with which the architect interacts—not only generates the

The Material

conditions within which to work, but is in fact the *place* itself in which and with which to operate.

In what way, then, is the work of 51N4E and RUF specifically useful to reflect on the state of practice and on the transformations taking place within architectural practice? 51N4E and RUF work in environments where conventional relationships between context and building, urban and rural, and temporary and permanent disintegrate, and where economic and social models have dramatically shifted in a few short decades. Their sites are territories of uncertainty, where it is difficult to decipher what the architect can control. Some of these are places where the profession itself does not exist.

Instead of confronting these uncertainties head on, 51N4E and RUF situate their practices amid a series of contextual questions: How do we design public space in a city like Tirana, where for decades a totalitarian regime stifled the very notion of private space? How do we imagine sustainable living in a city like Ulaanbaatar, devastated by coal pollution, where new residents in nomadic housing types make up 20 percent of the population? How do we reconceive the identities and spaces of the Chinese countryside, forgotten and excluded for centuries by social reforms and now quickly melding with the urban? How do we return the fragments of Brussels's failed utopian North District plan to the city?

Questions like these invite us to not only return to the archetypal problems of space production—what we designate as public or private, how we treat the air or light, how we define place—but to experiment with the present. In this present moment, the tools needed to answer these questions cannot simply be limited to the physical, material strategy of building. The answers must include the very elements that define context in its broadest form—people and institutions, economies and identities, charities and funding providers, politicians and clients, infrastructure and markets, crops and livestock, local technologies and global materials. If context is an assembly of things and agencies[3]—itself simultaneously a site and an instrument of that site's transformation—it is crucial to position the role of the architect as just one player within this ecology.

3   See Bruno Latour, "From Realpolitik to Dingpolitik or How to Make Things Public," in *Making Things Public: Atmospheres of Democracy*, eds. Bruno Latour and Peter Weibel (Karlsruhe & Cambridge, MA: ZKM and MIT Press, 2005), 14–43.

The Collision

As both insiders and outsiders, the architects of 51N4E and RUF act in turn as builders, planners, entrepreneurs, activists, community organizers, and policymakers. They are directors and activists, choreographers of relationships and conditions, and, from their liminal vantages, careful observers of what cannot—and, as their work shows, should not—be controlled. Taking this decentralized and dynamic position, the two offices provide a disciplinary reflection on the role of the architect as author. What they offer, in the face of a new, complex, and urbanized context, is a case for the radical power of an ethics of weakness. To redesign our present, ultimately, we have to be able to listen, observe, and strategically incorporate, absorb, and enable other actors' points of view. Only then does the building that emerges reflect what context means today, and only then does it meaningfully contribute to context's transformation.

DIALOGUE AS A SELF-REFLECTIVE MODEL

Listening, observing, and incorporating others' points of view are, more than utilitarian design strategies, key elements of dialogue, of exchange. How can we transform these dynamic, conversational elements—questions and reactions, positions and oppositions, silences and interferences, proximity and contrasts—into a coherent reflection on making architecture today? How can we imagine an architectural exhibition as, all at once, a form of dialogue and a representation of it? How can we design a conceptual space conducive to different ways of looking, thinking, and drawing architecture today in response to inscrutable and constantly shifting contexts?

The CCA's Manifesto series of exhibitions and books was conceived in 2006 to investigate the complexities of our time through architecture by bringing contemporary practices into conversation. Discussions between Gilles Clément and Philippe Rahm on redirecting our approach to the environment (2006); between Greg Lynn, Michael Maltzan, and Alessandro Poli on the meaning of the relationship between technique and technology (2010); between Stephen Taylor and Ryue Nishizawa on forms of living in dense urban fabrics (2008); between Bijoy Jain and Umberto Riva on the redefinition of the domestic "interior" (2014); and, most recently, between Kersten Geers, David Van Severen, and Go Hasegawa on the role and use of history in

The Traffic

architectural practice today (2017) have served as launching points for fifteen years of reflection on the themes most urgent and central to contemporary society.

Through the Manifesto series, the institution transforms into a backdrop for conversation, generating and inducing conditions for exchange, friction, and self-reflection in light of a chosen theme. Architects are invited to inhabit the space of dialogue, aware that the very nature of the format will transform the narratives they cast of their work into something new, shaped by multiple hands and eyes.

Now, with this last chapter, we end by exploring the relationships between the practice of architecture itself and the ecology of things around it. While previous CCA projects such as *The Other Architect* (2014) and *Our Happy Life* (2019) traced and investigated the multifaceted role of the architect and how it has transformed through the years, *The Things Around Us* intersects this research by exploring and analyzing the means, relational mechanisms, and tools the architect uses to move between the folds of complex political and socio-economic systems.

The Things Around Us does not revolve around the idea of an exhaustive presentation of 51N4E's and RUF's projects, but is structured like a catalogue of fragments, an atlas of strategies and tactics that can be used to intervene in moments of constant and dramatic territorial transformation. Thoughts, hypotheses, failures, and interventions at different scales are combined and layered to reflect the composite strategies that both offices use to investigate and transform places within the fissures of today's shifting contexts.

Conceived as a museum of notes and tools used in the field, *The Things Around Us* is the result of a year of cataloguing, discussions, journeys, and site visits. The architecture of 51N4E and RUF reveals itself in the project less as a series of finished objects than as the manifestation of a series of processes. Landing somewhere between question and reaction, proximity and contrast, assonance and distance, *The Things Around Us* is a manifesto of a position, the story of two approaches to context, and a testament to the very possibility of making architecture with and within context today.

The Studio

The Display

The Meeting

Where Meaning Can Emerge

51N4E in conversation with the CCA

(51N4E)

Sotiria Kornaropoulou
Aline Neirynck
Freek Persyn

(CCA)

Irene Chin
Francesco Garutti
Andrew Scheinman

1. RESTRUCTURING THE OFFICE

Francesco Garutti (CCA)

When we first met, in Brussels, you were telling me about the new structure of the office. What's behind the change?

Freek Persyn (51N4E)

The idea is that we're trying to create some clarity, to deal with the fact that 51N4E has gradually started to take up more and more diverse work. The name 51N4E has become a kind of symbol for an office that does a lot of things, but nobody really knows what. So, we've moved this name to a holding company that can facilitate and foster collaborations. It's a holding company in the sense that it "holds" very diverse activities and offers support for larger operational questions and dynamic and complex processes of transformation.

This new 51N4E contains different studios, each of which are in their own way about intervening in different moments of the process. One studio is called Cast. This, you could say, is the architectural company, focused on adaptive reuse, but also on transforming existing settlements. The goal here is to imagine and build environments that are inherently about adaptation, that have a capacity to absorb and facilitate change.

The second studio is called Acte, and with this studio the idea is to focus more on the conditions that create projects, on setting the right conditions. It's also about creating alliances and developing business models. Sometimes, in an architectural project, we're asked to deliver an answer to a question that's not even properly posed. Sometimes it is better to activate a second track that deals with the questions that emerge in the process. Often, we also feel not enough people are involved; we want to include people that are too often left out of the "urban transformation process."

Sotiria Kornaropoulou (51N4E)

You can also see this transformation less as restructuring than as giving form to what is already happening, especially with these first two studios. Cast, the studio with the architectural focus, has been growing quickly. Giving it autonomy is one way to manage its growth. We need to professionalize certain aspects of the architectural projects,

The Maintenance

streamline their processes, dive deeper into circularity, adaptive re-use. And then with the creation of Acte, we can continue to work on the conditions of the project by asking questions, putting together coalitions of actors, programming, testing basic relations between space and context. We wanted to give this work visibility because, while subtle, it has a lot of weight in determining what happens in the projects that follow. Splitting companies is also in this sense an op-portunity to take this second line of work more seriously, to develop its tools and methods.

And then the third studio—though this is still more of a dream than a real company—is called Root. It's about making environments more biodiverse, about working with plants both inside and outside. It is a bit of an experiment for us because it is the first one that im-plies a structural collaboration with a party outside the 51N4E circle. It started with one successful collaboration with the people we worked with on Skanderbeg Square.

Persyn

What was for us very interesting in that collaboration was that these people are actually contractors. They do landscape design but have backgrounds in biology and ecology, and they come to it from a con-tracting perspective. They focus on how to install things, how to maintain them. They don't start with a totally new design. In this way, landscape design with them becomes more like maintenance design. It's about growing landscape in a certain direction rather than in-stalling and planting it from scratch. That's where this third studio comes from.

Kornaropoulou

We come to the table with different backgrounds and expertise, but we share an attitude. Working together on Skanderbeg Square, we discussed how the square could be in one, five, twenty, or fifty years. For us, this was very refreshing: though architecture is much more inert than landscape, we would still not really dare to guess how con-ditions will change in the next fifty years. From both sides, what we tried to set up is a solid base with a generous internal logic to leave margins for change. In the process, we realized how much landscape is defined by the way it is followed up on and managed. We would often show up with design references only to realize that what we were look-ing for was more a question of how long the grass grows than what our design looked like.

So, we have plenty of reasons to move ahead with these struc-tural shifts, but it has taken a while to figure out how exactly to tie it all together.

Persyn

The most complex projects we aspire to will always be collaborations between the three studios, but each studio will develop its own ex-pertise and be able to facilitate a change or expansion of the scope of any particular project. It's a new way to deal with complexity and with the fact that in given contexts you are confronted with things that you don't get to steer. If you work with a situation that has its own con-straints and its own reality rather than just a brief, you have to work your way around it. You have to work with it.

Kornaropoulou

Over the last ten years, we've also gradually established a less hierar-chical way of working, more team- and network-based, so the change will help accommodate that horizontal structure.

Garutti

Was this restructuring a reaction to the contexts you work in? Could we say that fifteen years in Tirana, Albania—a context dom-inated by economic uncertainties, evolving ambitions, sociopolit-ical frictions, and a profound sense of mutual trust with citizens, contractors, and clients—influenced your approach to practice? Did you take this back from Albania to Brussels?

Persyn

Yeah, in a way, we're formalizing something we've had to do time and again. The restructuring is about learning from situations that we're confronted with. Time and again, we'd noticed that we had to take care not just of the answer but of the conditions of the project. Of course, splitting the office up, we risk segmenting it into a modernistic orga-nization where everyone has their own expertise and no one talks to each other. That's the danger of this model. But for us, the advantage is that different perspectives are embodied by different people. Complexity is literally represented at the table.

So yes, in a way, it's an answer to our working with these different contexts and different situations. If you don't want to just project a concept onto a situation but to learn from it, you have to work with it and be informed by it.

A good example of this, I think, is in the North District of Brussels, where simple solutions have proven, in our time working there, very difficult to enact. Take all of these hostile and unattractive ground floors in the area's modernist towers. Architecturally, it would be very simple to turn them into active ground floors. You don't have to be a wizard to imagine how to do that. So why doesn't it happen? It has to do with the constellation of actors, with how things are managed, with how expectations are built, with how policy is steered. You have to work through different processes than just architectural ones to unlock these situations. Things are actually very organised, but they don't come together: you have cleaners, facility managers, security people, receptionists, plant caretakers, etc. but no one is really looking at how what all of these people do works toward something bigger. Our society often engineers its own fragmentation. That's where Acte as a studio can play a role.

Our work in Albania was, in a sense, a crash course in looking at aspects beyond the architectural, in becoming aware of how a society organizes itself. We were very young when we arrived and were taken very seriously and given a lot of responsibility. In a way, being so young, we were in a position to embrace that responsibility: more established firms treated it as more of a funny side project that could work but also could not. We took it overly seriously, and so, in that sense, we were also growing up in public. Inevitably, we fell, and then we got up again.

Garutti
So what made you stay there?

Persyn
What was amazing in Tirana was that people really want something—they have a dream. They want to grow and become better. And even if the process is often extremely clumsy, it's so sincere. In this way, it's

so different than what you see in Belgium, where people are forced into a position in which they can only check boxes. In Western Europe, people have their professional responsibilities. When they give you a commission, they have often figured out what is needed beforehand, and that's what they give you to work on as architects. There's no room to manoeuvre at all. Tirana is a place where people start from a sense of direction, an intuition almost, and they give you the space to shape that. It's a huge opportunity. You find can find a similar quality in the open call, the competition procedure in Flanders and now also in Brussels: it favours a similar type of openness.

Garutti

Was the new political situation in Albania part of the appeal?

Persyn

Yes. We were immediately fascinated by the way people live outside and use the city as a place to meet. Edi Rama—who, as mayor of Tirana, started this whole dynamic—wanted to make citizens by making public space. He saw the city as the environment that produces citizens and not the other way around. So we as young architects had a very intuitive link with him.

Kornaropoulou

This is something that the restructuring alone will not change—the need to have parties on the client side who are looking for the same things. Part of the reason to structure the company differently is to allow for clarity in what we are trying to achieve so that a good match can be more than just a happy accident.

2. MODESTY AND FLEXIBILITY

Andrew Scheinman (CCA)

It sounds like you've you've made a point to hold onto a youthful seriousness or naivete, a kind of happy uncertainty. What does it mean for you to be uncertain or to be naive? What are you listening to and what sort of noise do you just let roll past you?

Persyn

It's about giving yourself the time to look at something and see how it speaks to you rather than pushing or projecting onto it. Allowing a bit of space. If you look at it with fresh eyes without projecting, then you come to understand certain things. The work speaks back to you. And that's why it's often slow. You have to make things or produce things, externalize them, and give yourself the possibility to verify what you find and what you see.

Aline Neirynck (51N4E)

It's interesting to see new contexts first and foremost as testing grounds for opportunities, for setting up experiences and observing how people react to them. It's interesting to take time for decisions. You set up a situation, take a step back, and look at how things play out.

Irene Chin (CCA)

So in these new contexts, you act as outsiders, observing first. But what about in Brussels? How do you find gaps or look with fresh eyes and distance in your own home?

Persyn

The funny thing is that in Brussels we are to an extent outsiders as well. French is not our native tongue, but a lot of people in the administration and in political decision-making processes are French speakers. There's an establishment of architects in Brussels that speak as a kind of unit. We're not perceived as being very interesting. Up until quite recently, when we applied to competitions, we were told our work was rigid and not very urban. There were some harsh critiques.

Gradually, of course, we became less of outsiders, but there are still certain circles in Brussels that are very hard for us to reach. Unlike

Tirana, which is very small and where you can get to know people quite easily, Brussels is quite complex, very layered. We are in a way a minority in our own city.

When we did the competition for the tower at the World Trade Center, we teamed up with l'AUC from Paris both for their outside perspective and because they have a French-speaking team. By having this international office work with us, we would have someone who could speak the language, but also someone who could destabilize the contrast between our Flemish backgrounds and the French-speaking clients and decision-makers. Belgium is a bit caught up in this binary opposition between two languages. So, in that sense, Brussels is a bit of a city of outsiders, I think. Or becoming more and more of one.

Kornaropoulou

In terms of demographics, outsiders are the only majority in Brussels. I heard on a radio program recently that there are only two countries in the world that are not represented in the nationalities of Brussels's inhabitants. A lot of people find it very easy to belong here. But then, at the same time, it's very difficult to navigate how the city is run. It's very complex for its size.

Neirynck

I strongly believe that the city of Brussels is one of the reasons why our team is so diverse. The fact that Brussels is the capital of Europe makes it interesting to work in as a context. Brussels does not have a clear identity, and that's why it will always attract different personalities. Somehow the office tries to mimic Brussels. We create common ground in what we want to achieve by taking different people's perspectives into account, by learning how to be modest and adapting ourselves to the many opinions and wishes at the table.

Chin

Even within Brussels, you've operated as a bit of a nomadic office. Can you tell us about the idea of the site as a temporary office, as at the World Trade Center, where, in 2017, you moved your office into one of the two towers? What does it mean to be on the ground, both literally and metaphorically?

Persyn

It has been really, really enriching, this thing we tried. If you look at the North District, you can see that doing something there will take decades. You can't expect to do something there in a few years. It's so dramatic and so problematic and so complex. But being there, you start to discover a lot of possibilities and links, you understand how things work, and you start to see this place from different perspectives. You see it as a daily environment, but you also see it as a conceptual environment. You imagine how it would be in twenty years.

Moving to the North District also changed the way we saw ourselves and how we operated. When you have your own office, the office is as big as your organization. Often it happens that if you move into a bigger office space, your office grows. You could almost manage the size of your office by choosing the site. The experiment in the North District was to move to a place where we could test out working with other companies, where we could test the limits of our organization. In that sense, the move at once grounded us and put us in a very open place.

Kornaropoulou

I think this has been a two-part experiment: we've been on the ground in the sense that we've put ourselves inside this area in transition, but we've also tried a different approach to office space. To a certain extent this brought on more logistical considerations, but it also opened up many more possibilities and a different way of looking at ourselves. The restructuring, the working in a network—these are fragments of the same dynamic.

The Language

Neirynck

Having an open space that is easily adaptable, where things can easily move to fit our needs, is very interesting. The adaptable and movable furniture with which we try to create either more or less intimate spaces, where our clients and collaborators feel comfortable to speak up and design together toward a common goal—it's very important. Going to the North District opened up these possibilities for us.

Scheinman

Can I ask briefly just why it would take years to get anything accomplished in the North District in Brussels? Why is it so dramatic?

Persyn

It's dramatic because it—well, first of all, it has been traumatic. Fifty years ago, a whole neighbourhood was flattened, with many, many people evicted, all for an ambitious project that failed almost from the very start. The idea had been to transform a fragment of this mid-nineteenth-century industrial neighborhood into a kind of European Manhattan, with curtain-wall buildings. For years, the area was vacant, and the way it has finally taken shape feels like a huge disappointment. It's a space that no one really likes, that everyone despises. Imagine an airport or business park in the city centre—it's that same level of urbanity and of inclusion.

But it's also very symbolic because of this trauma and because of its built matter. For the twenty years I'd lived in Brussels, nothing was really happening in the North District. Its development was at a standstill. Three years ago, when Dieter Leyssen and I were playing around with the idea of doing something with the district, Brussels's *bouwmeester*, or Chief Architect, told us, "Sometimes you have places in the city that no one is really interested in. They're monofunctional, yeah, but that's it. That's how life is." It was matter-of-fact acceptance of failure, which is of course understandable when you look at all of the challenges Brussels is facing. He was choosing his battles, and in the last few decades, the North District was never a political priority. It is considered a space fucked up by real estate developers, people who extracted profit from the area and who should now deal with the problems. That is how politicians communicated about it. We jumped

The Developers

into a policy vacuum, you could say. So yes, it does take decades. Our tower project will take five years to build and even then, it's just one of the buildings in the district. If you want to create another sense of life in a place, one building is not enough.

Garutti

But then you're also working on another iconic building in the area, the IBM tower, no? Inhabiting, deconstructing, reimagining, and redesigning these two modern monoliths in relation to their contexts, you're redeveloping the whole area.

Persyn

In that sense we have been, at least in the North District, hugely successful. Beyond our expectations. We're working on the IBM tower because we've shown that we can handle the renovation of these buildings and that we offer a different approach than just redoing the façade. The developers of DWNTWN were interested in that. They want to challenge the current real estate market in Brussels, but they're also looking for alternate, more circular ways of building. In that sense, our mindsets align.

Garutti

So the design is more like a physical representation of a dialogue—a dialogical construction. Sometimes you're the centre, driving the project, and sometimes you're on the outside. Sometimes you're coordinating relationships. Do you consciously reflect on this change—on the changing position of the architect?

Persyn

Yeah, for sure. For instance, the job we have for the World Trade Center in Brussels's North District is just a percentage of the commission. There's the main architect from Jasper-Eyers, a big firm in Brussels, and then we complement. The way for us to survive in this construction is to come up with a vision, a strong proposal, a new approach, and therefore a new identity for the building. But we also think about how our proposal could work with a business-as-usual approach, how we could use construction methods or materials already commonly used by Jasper-Eyers. We think about what could be different, but also about what could remain the same. In that sense, we do think about the role we play. Or rather, about what the situation asks of us. So yes, it is strategic, what we do, and often about choreographing ourselves and, if possible, others, along with the process itself. In that process, we act accordingly and pragmatically to see what can emerge.

Chin

Tell us about how you adapt this role from large-scale projects like the North District of Brussels and Skanderbeg Square in Tirana to more intimate designs, like the tables at the Center for Openness and Dialogue and the love seats in Skanderbeg, or the single family house of Room in the City in Leuven.

Kornaropoulou

This summer we were involved in a temporary intervention, a mobile forest, with the Lab North initiative in the North District, and it plays with this contrast between big and small. The extra-large sidewalks in the area make for all these blind façades, but they are also but they are also huge reserves of space. Installing a lot of plants, a bit of water, some benches and tables can transform the experience of the place. You see people slowing down. Some take a seat, some hesitate. It's something unusual in the area.

Persyn

Space can reveal how people want to behave. It produces certain conditions you respond to. But these examples are in spaces that don't tell you how to behave. They don't reveal those behavioural patterns quite so obviously. The love chairs are too big for one person and too small for two, so people decide for themselves how to manage their interpersonal distances. We can't decide it for them.

Somehow discomfort can offer a lot of freedom. You're not automatically reduced to a consumer. Discomfort allows you to take a position. This is a discussion we often have in our process: what kind of freedom does the design trigger? Freedom comes not only from giving people convenient choices, but from putting people in a position to choose for themselves.

Garutti

Deciding what to control or not to control seems key to your approach to making space. Choosing to design the most specific constraints allows, paradoxically, for openness—that is, openness either in the design process or in use. You create infrastructure that produces a sort of emotional proximity.

Persyn

Yes, and the way we work, it's a constant struggle, but it's a struggle that has become a strategy. We've often found ourselves in situations where we have to give up control and where we can't design from A to Z, so we've had to become strategic about which things we choose to change. We look for small changes, for interventions or even disruptions that can colour everything else. With the love seats, there is other furniture in the square—concrete benches outnumber the chairs by a lot—but the chairs produce so much meaning that they start to colour everything around them.

Kornaropoulou

The design of the love chair started as a vague idea of mobile furniture on the square. It was pitched early on in the discussions with the city, but only became a reality toward the end of the project. There was, of course, a lot of doubt about whether it was a good idea to invest in mobile furniture in a public space that's not fenced off at night and cannot be really controlled. But it was so clear what possibilities it would open up. So the uniqueness of the design became a necessity. You can't just grab a chair and take it home: it would be too obvious where it came from. The strategy was to create flexibility where there usually is none, enabling and disabling options, playing with expectations. With small-scale designs, you can do that more directly.

Neirynck

That's why adaptability is so important. Take a project like the BUDA Art Factory. With such a small budget, we focused on the basics of what the building should offer: a visual identity from the street, smart circulation, and a range of different spaces. After it was completed, the project still kept transforming: the client added to what we had framed. Users build their own emotional connections over time.

Scheinman

There's this clear emotional level, something about human connection, that you convey in talking about these projects. Your book *How Things Meet* even begins with a short story with fictional protagonists, and at the ETH lab where you teach, there's a theatre set where students are invited to perform. Would it be fair to say that the way you think through and present these works, both to us now and to clients in process, is itself a strategy? Is it a means of coyly suggesting and exploring new ideas?

Persyn

How Things Meet is a very different story from ETH. *How Things Meet* came out of frustration. We didn't know how to communicate our work in Albania. It also had to do with an ongoing discussion we were having in the office about the value of work. Johan Anrys—another founding partner of 51N4E—and I never wanted to be dismissive of the parts of our work that have failed. We wanted to show these failings as something valuable, as experiences that we learn from. Those failures can be very disarming. But looking at a portfolio, you assume that everything shown is something you consider good. With *How Things Meet*, you get the fiction and then the timeline, and in this timeline, it becomes clear that the work is more about learning. The story there was more about communicating what we were doing, including the messy or unresolved stuff. It was a way to start to relate the questions that came out of that complexity.

Garutti

In *How Things Meet*, you don't just present projects, but the stories of those projects as ecosystems of actors and events, conditions and atmospheres, mistakes and achievements. You also use this narrative approach in process with your clients. How do you use narrative as a tool in the design process?

Chin

Even with us, yeah. You sent us a conceptual design proposal for the show in the form of a narrative.

Persyn

Yeah, that's true. I hadn't considered that. A narrative is also about trying to forecast an experience: it's projecting that experience, imagining it beforehand.

Garutti

To me, it's about curating the conditions for openness and dialogue and about making a kind of design infrastructure that sticks around after you leave. About not overdetermining the future of a place and instead modifying the conditions, allowing the transformation to take place without you.

Kornaropoulou

That's a nice way to put it.

Persyn

We want to enable situations, to do one thing in the hope that a second thing will follow. I have a feeling a lot of architects only focus on that first thing and that's where their design process stops. But our work is not about giving that kind of order. It's about creating connections, trying to trigger something.

5. TIMELINES AND LIFESPANS

Garutti

This makes me think of the idea of curating a building, rather than just designing it.

Neirynck

We do have that kind of a relationship with the BUDA factory. We've followed up and have changed the building and modified it, made new openings and new connections. And it's interesting because you start to structure these changes collectively, with the clients and the users, to build preciousness and an identity. You discuss together what to respect and to keep and what to allow to transform according to its daily use.

Persyn

The TID tower is the same. It's very mathematical, its façade seems to be coherent, but really, if you look at it, the building is ad hoc. Only two small things are defined, and everything else is negotiable. There is the shape of the tower, the space of the golden cupola and the urban void of the galleria. Everything around these interventions has been malleable. In retrospect, it is amazing to see how much these three shapes have been respected and how much the things between them have been changed. There's room to play around these things. You define a timeframe in which certain things hold and others change. Architecture has this capacity to structure different timeframes like this, and at certain moments it can even stop time.

Chin

Are there limitations to participatory processes like these?

Persyn

In Dutch, dialogue is *tegenspraak*—something like "counter-speech," which has a certain resistance baked into it. It's true that participation has this kind of "go with the flow" notion attached to it, the idea that you should make people as happy as possible and talk as much as possible. Of course, there's something good about it, something noble. But dialogue is also about resistance and about silence. When you don't speak, you can listen to what's not being said. The word participation, for me, too often treats citizens like customers or consumers: their desires should be met, and the best design is the one that meets the most desires, or worse still, leaves everyone in their comfort zones.

We try to do two things: one is to understand what a person wants, their ambitions and their capacity for complexity. The second is to take responsibility for exceeding that situation, to bring it to a higher level. In participatory practice, this doesn't always seem like the goal.

Kornaropoulou

I think the best dialogues have people commenting afterward that what we arrived at was not at all what they expected. We ourselves are also surprised when something new emerges. Not every meeting gets there, and it does take a lot of energy and openness from everyone, but when it happens it is something magical.

Garutti

Does the process change entirely with each project? Or do you have a set of tools or constraints you use to enact this dialogue?

Persyn

Johan is very good at trying the bad ideas of others. That's often your first reaction in this process, that the idea is bad. But if you try it, you end up levelling yourself with the others. Then you start to understand what it means. You sometimes discover things you hadn't thought about yourself. It's good to give the other person the benefit of the doubt.

Scheinman

Could you tell us a bit more about your connection to ETH Zurich and the Design in Dialogue Lab there? How did that come about, and how does it feed back into your practice?

Persyn

It was quite an intuitive choice to apply there: I'd heard it was a school that creates the conditions for you to be entrepreneurial. My application was based on a proposal of what I wanted to investigate, and, in that sense, if they hadn't liked the proposal I wouldn't have worked there. The conditions the school offers are, I think, unique in Europe. I often have the feeling that what we do at 51N4E doesn't have a good conceptual framework—there are no real words for it—so I was intrigued to develop it more. Our approach is, I feel, quite different, and so I hope that ETH allows me to both describe it and develop it.

The Boundaries

6. THE DYNAMICS OF PROCESS

Chin

I'd like to end us on this idea of transformation and on the urban today. The default way of seeing the forces that define the urban today would be to put -isms or -ion words on it—words like global-ization—which seem to oversimplify its complexity.

Persyn

I was talking before about architecture as a process—things have become so interrelated and interconnected that you do indeed get degrees between urban and rural, city and not city. These still do ex-ist as environments. You can feel one way in one place and another way in another place. In a Belgian city, there's a certain density of so-cial interaction that you won't find in more suburban areas. But the processes underlying the dynamics in each of these places are inter-related. It's more interesting to look at these similar processes and patterns than to think in categories.

And then, how do you intervene? If everything is a process, how do you intervene? For me, there's a conceptual flattening that's nec-essary, a process of looking at things in a fresh way that's applicable wherever you are.

Scheinman

Does that add up to a kind of methodology? The approach you've outlined about listening and creating the conditions for a dia-logue—is that specific to the places that you've worked, or do you think it could be used wherever?

Persyn

What's specific, maybe, is the awareness, the way you understand your own impact. There's not an unchanged or unchanging reality out there, so the fact that you intervene in a site gives you an agency that changes the conditions you work in. When you make a building, you are not just making it fit into a context, but you actively change that context, especially in areas that are not very consolidated, that are in doubt or in transformation. The same goes for a group dynamic in a project. You shape it while it also shapes you. In a way, ideally, it is everyone's responsibility to attend to both sides of the equation at once. If you want to understand the dynamics and how to work with them, it's better to slow down than to speed up, which is very contradictory to urbanization processes today. If you can let go of the idea or the anxiety that you are there to defend your own stake or to push for your agenda, it is often easier to see how all the stakes can be connected, reframed, or integrated into a bigger whole. Those moments, where meaning can emerge, are what we also try to design.

Choreography Is a Good Word for It

Rural Urban Framework in conversation with the CCA

(RUF)
Joshua Bolchover
John Lin

(CCA)
Irene Chin
Francesco Garutti
Andrew Scheinman

1. APPROACHING CONTEXT

Andrew Scheinman (CCA)

In your research, you've alluded to your interest in revisiting some of the sites Bernard Rudofsky looked at in his 1964 *Architecture Without Architects* show at the Museum of Modern Art, which featured anonymously authored buildings like the underground houses of rural China. For Rudofsky, these rural sites were defined by their informal and unselfconscious architecture. But as you wrote, these sites are radically different today, characterized by "abandonment, infrastructural collisions, mutations, adaptations, and contested territories—rapid urbanization either directly or indirectly having an impact." You argue that "the vernacular, the anonymous, and the rural need to be considered through a new narrative that accounts for the intrusion of global development onto vast territories of land."

John Lin (RUF)

I think this statement underscores an approach to the issue of context. These contextual changes and transformations are happening—and happening more and more rapidly. As architects, we try to both catch up to the speed of transformation and reconnect with aspects of history and of culture. We're interested in looking forward in time, but we do this specifically as a consequence of how we look backward in time.

It also underscores an awareness of our roles as architects. We're not just interested in shaping context and understanding context, but in allowing context to consciously shape how we work. How can we rethink our profession? On the one hand, it's a matter of working in places where the profession doesn't really exist, or at least rarely exists, but it's also a matter of asking why it's so difficult for the profession to exist in these areas. That's what attracts us to working in rural China and in the capital of Mongolia.

Joshua Bolchover (RUF)

We're also interested in unpicking some of the terminology used. When Rudofsky was making his show, terms like "vernacular," "the rural," and "the urban" had very clear meanings. That's clearly changed, so for us to look at what defines the rural today and what defines the urban becomes critical. Have these terms become outdated? At a lot of the sites we visit, that's a driving question. What is the vernacular in China? What does it mean? Why is it relevant? How do places or contexts evolve? How do these sites deal with the pressures of the present, and how can they begin to anticipate the future? Our projects try to work with these dynamics, to understand how they touch the ground, shape space, and configure territory.

Francesco Garutti (CCA):
So Rudofsky was something like a lesson or a tool for you.

Bolchover
Rudofsky's examples describe strong and coherent forms based on the local intelligence of available materials, craft, and climate. Forms of settlement are models of growth and adaptation that remain fascinating and relevant today. Contemporary urban forces have completely disrupted and altered these territories. Rudofsky gathered, catalogued, and described what he saw in his photographs or in photographs by others.

We are still interested in how these material forms of architecture can emerge from their contexts, but I think we're also adding another layer of thinking about what else forms those contexts. What are the other political and economic conditions and forces that begin to shape territory?

2. PLACES THAT DON'T NEED ARCHITECTS

Irene Chin (CCA)

You describe the starting point of your work together as the enaction of the Chinese government's policy, in 2005, of urbanizing the country's rural regions. That's really the contemporary pressure we're talking about here, right? Tell us about what interested you about these places to begin with. How did you end up in both the rural areas of the Pearl River Delta and the ger districts of Ulaanbaatar?

Lin

When we started in rural China in 2006, architects were primarily working in cities. There was a kind of excitement about the high-speed urban experiment. We happened upon the rural and realized the same transformations were happening in the rural in very different ways. We could see radical changes even in these very remote villages, and so we tried to figure out how we could possibly work there. But we did not "exit" the urban; we are still a part of that large experiment. Same thing in Mongolia. There's this fascination we have with areas that seem to resist, just a little, the formal participation of the architect.

Bolchover

Although we're interested in the forces that shape context and, therefore, in the relationship between architecture and those forces, it's a misconception to think that we are attempting to change those forces directly. The architecture we make does not solve the economic, health, or social problems endemic in the places where we work. It's more about understanding how architecture is positioned within the network of these other forces shaping it. We're acting with an understanding that, within this network, the spaces we make can trigger and enable new programs, infrastructures, or social relationships to take place.

Going back to context and why we looked at these particular sites: I think John is absolutely right on why we started looking at these places that were resisting conventional forms of urbanization—these pockets of anomalies or contradictions that fascinated us. But also,

The Law

what I think was fascinating about these places is that they challenged fundamentally what it means to make architecture at these sites. We had to deal with the essential questions we assumed we knew the answer to based on what we understood the words "urban" and "rural" to mean. We had to reset our understanding and preconceptions and ask: If all of these things are up for grabs, how do we then begin to work with these conditions?

Both Mongolia and China gave us opportunities to rethink: What does rural mean? What does urban mean? What does it mean to make a place? How do we make it? What materials do we use? How do we interact with labour and the local villages? And in that regard, both Mongolia and China represented a sort of primordial soup, a moment when things are about to emerge from the mud. All the pieces are there, the pressure is there, the dynamics are there. It's this moment of emergence that underlies our interest in those sites.

Lin

It almost feels like we're inviting ourselves to a party. We're interested in these situations where we're not invited through specific commissions. And so, when you have to invite yourself—when you have to create the new conditions and assemble the pieces and the dynamics for how to fund the work and what problems to resolve—I think you begin to work differently with context. It challenges us to reach in at a deeper level, first by addressing whether we, as architects, are even needed. Sometimes, we've simply walked away.

But when it is successful, it really comes out of a certain dynamic involving various people and stakeholders— something we've helped orchestrate. For me, that's really the architectural project. We discover ways for these groups to come together, and the architecture is simply the evidence of that, an artifact.

Our fascination with these contexts goes beyond the physical. People think about architecture and context as a physical condition or place, and we're digging deeper, trying to redefine context as a set of forces.

Bolchover

Both the Mongolian and Chinese contexts bring to light some of the serious and critical issues we're likely to face in the future. You look at Mongolia and you see it as the developing world, but it could also be an apocalyptic version of future life. Everyone is living with extraordinary air pollution, no one has access to clean water, the soil's becoming toxic, and no one can afford homes to live in. You begin to question whether this is specific to Mongolia or a vision of the future. Or in China, the urbanization process has created vast agglomerations of non-urban territory with generic forms of housing. You can already find this condition the world over. Is this what we're going to get everywhere?

These are highly specific situations on the one hand, but, I believe, they can also shed light on what's taking place around the world as the processes of urbanization take hold and co-opt rural territory. There are lessons there, but it's not our role to read the lessons so pedagogically or didactically. Through the process of making architecture, situations and approaches emerge that we can learn from.

Lin

Nowhere on earth is isolated enough to be outside the general forces of urbanization that shape our society. But the places we are working in offer new pathways. We're interested in their remoteness—not just in the geographical sense, but a remoteness from the standardized notion of urbanity in which the vast majority of the world lives and works. We're interested in finding new possibilities in remote places.

Chin

Can you tell us a bit about the specifics of not being part of the conversation to begin with? How do you gain access?

Lin

Well, we can start from the very beginning, with how we started to work, in 2005. The Chinese government created a nine-year compulsory education system, and at the same time, it required the building of many schools, typically in rural areas. The term *xi wang xiao xue*, directly translated as "hope school," became an emblem, inviting donors and foreign charities to help fund the construction of primary schools in remote areas throughout China.

In our first project, we were approached by a charity that had already built around one hundred of these schools. They were built in the exact same way, and the charity began to notice certain kinds of disappointments, maybe even failures, with how these schools were eventually utilized. At the same time, this charity was very interested in promoting notions of ecology and sustainability and asked us to develop a pilot project in Guangdong Province.

The project happened to be about a twelve-hour drive from Hong Kong, through Shenzhen, Dongguan, and many other second- and third-tier cities and towns. This journey—the experience of going from Hong Kong to China through alternating urban and rural territories—piqued our interest in the process of urbanization and helped us establish Rural Urban Framework as a geopolitical project.

We began to realize that many of the charities building schools in China came from Hong Kong, and they had a lot of money to build schools. They had money for bricks and building materials, but they didn't have any funding for design. At the same time, there was an increasing sense of disillusionment with the projects that were being built. Through our positions in the university, we leveraged what we recognized as a research possibility with the ability to offer design services to these charities. We discovered a potential ecology in which research activities, cultural interests, and government policies aligned. By combining two funding models—academic grants and

The Charities

charity donations—we were able to achieve something that nobody in the profession or in academia was doing.

Bolchover

There's a second chapter to that. John is referring to the school that he did in Qinmo. After they built the new school he had designed, there was an opportunity to deal with the school that had been abandoned, the old school building. Through designing the new school, through actively going to the village many times and thinking about these sites, thinking about what was happening, observing the construction of new houses despite the abandonment in the village, we started to think about the old school. The old school was where this idea of doing architecture through enabling and working with a network of stakeholders and actors really emerged.

The question was what to do with it. We could come up with our own brief. It was a very simple project. The idea was for it to be a teaching facility that could host several summer camps to help kids learn English and improve their Chinese and maths. An agricultural institute in Hong Kong, the Kadoorie Institute, also collaborated with us to convert the courtyard into a garden and greenhouse to grow high-income-yielding crops and to demonstrate more sustainable methods of pig and chicken farming. It was also a place for the community to gather for village meetings, for lion-dance practice, and an after-school club. The project tried to do many things. Not all of them were successful, but it was about pulling together these different networks of actors—the Kadoorie Institute, for example—and about the longer-term ecology of what this place would mean to the village. Once the kids had been through their education in the new school, they would then revisit and become the next generation of volunteer teachers, assisting the younger children during education camps in the old school.

We were trying to think of the old school as a node that would have various different impacts and effects in the community. Whether they were successful or not didn't really matter. What mattered was that we started to think of architecture as a site that enabled different networks to begin to overlap and influence actions and activities in that place. In many ways, the project was fundamental to our future thinking and ambitions for the architecture we were making.

Garutti

So, the architecture somehow positioned itself within the—you use the word "ecology."

Bolchover

Yes, the old school was a part of an ecology: an ecology of education, of agriculture, of economy. Yet the idea wasn't that the architecture would solve the economic problem by breeding a black chicken that could sell for twice as much as a regular chicken. The aim was that the building could become a site for pilot projects and educational exchange that would incubate new ideas, influencing the ecologies that the village was part of.

Lin

At the time, we were in the habit of working with a network of donors instead of one single client. We weren't quite conscious of the implications—we were just trying to do projects as young architects. We realized that, by bringing together various funding parties and stakeholders so that there is no obvious person in charge, the architect takes on a role of leadership. It's no longer just the traditional one-to-one relationship of client versus architect. After our first project, this became our established way of working. It helped us expand the role of the architect.

Scheinman

Is it a leadership among actors, or a director, or—is the design process in these new contexts more about mediation? Is design itself even central?

Lin

Jörg Stollmann once told me about an orchestra that tried to make music without a conductor. That story really stuck with me and resonated with many of the experiences we've had.

Bolchover

Yeah, it's sort of in between. I like that, "conductor." But we're also finding the band members too, right? It's not as if there's already an orchestra. We're piecing it together. Or testing which instruments we need in order to put on a performance. It's a good word. Others might be "enabler" or "curator." I'm not sure. "Leader" is not quite the right word. It has to be someone who can speculate how the future might unfold but can then put the right people together to allow for that scenario to take shape.

Garutti

It's interesting how the notion of failure could be a part of this. You prepare a set of possibilities. You define a framework and develop a methodology that responds to it.

Lin

Methodology is important because the architect works with many different projects and clients, many different conditions and physical sites and budgets. The architect has to tie all of these things together, and the way they do that can result in a single expression of architecture. When we say we're interested in certain types of sites, we're not actually looking for them; they simply have qualities we're attracted to. They're always at the periphery of the urbanization process, often on the frontlines, whether it's the rural village in China or the urban ger districts around Ulaanbaatar.

These are the qualities that tie our work together. I don't think we have a very strong or top-down, formal methodology for practice. In many ways, we're resistant to it. But we believe the final expression of the building is very important—it manifests the experience of collaboration and attests to the ability of competing agencies to find common ground.

Bolchover

I think the word "methodology" implies a set way of working with a set of tools. You conduct an experiment, get results, you write up the results, and then you try and evolve those somehow. The clearest example is when we did the Rural Urban Framework panorama, which was at the 2015 Chicago Architecture Biennial. That was a methodology, right? We went out, we took photographs, we observed the territory that we were moving through. We then synthesised them, processed

The Observations

them, and came up with a panorama which led us into dividing the territory into distinct parts. It was a methodology not for doing architecture, but for synthesising our thoughts about the things we were observing, writing about them, and thinking about how our work related to the different conditions we were witnessing. It was a methodology for research and for framing our understanding, not for design.

But I also think we need to be careful about how we use these terms. I think you said methodology can mean the network of actors, the ecology, the approach. I don't think it is.

Lin

Yeah, I don't think methodology is really the right word. Perhaps the right term is something that expresses an ability to react to unforeseen circumstances, like the idea of a strategy.

Bolchover

Methodology implies something quite fixed for me. The shift, the change in approach we make with different actors, how we begin to insert ourselves into these contexts or how we begin to intervene and bring actors together—I think it's important. It is a framework. Whether it's a vernacular structure, a hybrid house made of concrete and wood or a ger in a polluted environment, we react to what's already there.

5. UNCERTAINTY AND CONTROL

Garutti

Your methodological approach begins by considering the "uncertain" as the first tool you operate with. In this sense, your architecture seems to me to be about mediation. You start by considering the uncertainties of site conditions, adhering to the realities of the place and engaging in a dialogue. You mediate between communities, between politicians and villagers, between large-scale forces and local constraints, between the vernacular and what comes from elsewhere. Only then do you set the conditions for intervention.

Lin

Maybe it is the balance between control and its opposite. And this leads us to the idea of compromise and why it's such a necessary part of the process of making architecture. We can understand compromise as a process that occurs when other people and agencies try to take ownership of the project. This should be encouraged.

Scheinman

Sure, but what do we talk about when we talk about uncertainty and a lack of control? How do you decide what to control or not to control?

Bolchover

It's really about going into a project knowing that you can't control everything. Which already differentiates us from a majority of architects, who of course want to design everything and control everything. In the contexts in which we work, it's impossible to control everything. Once you get to the point where you acknowledge you can't, you are, on the one hand, liberated, but then you have to ask yourself: what is it that you want to orchestrate within the project? What can you control?

I think what we could control is the process, the organization. Where the light fittings are and how the wall meets the ground and whether there's a shadow gap or not doesn't really matter. It's about trying to figure out what key element of the project we want to maintain. For a lot of our projects, we only learned this through the act of building.

Lin

You're alluding to a repositioning of our values. We don't necessarily measure ourselves by how much we're able to control the site or the building process, which is what we've been taught in schools of ar-chitecture. Instead we try to define the line between what we design and what we don't. You could say this is an economical approach to architecture. Not just in financial terms, but in design effort. It's about finding out where design is most effective and what other parts can be resolved more generically.

The Compromise

6. CHOREOGRAPHY AND PARTICIPATION

The Bricks

Garutti

So, for example, the local production of the brick moulds for your Angdong hospital project and the collective construction of the pavers for your Taiping village bridge project: these small design choices end up not only contributing to the local economy, but becoming devices for community engagement.

Lin

Yes, we do engage builders directly. The moulds are built by contractors along with labourers from the village. Both groups contribute their own ideas, and we rethink our design process continually to incorporate these ideas. This engagement directly impacts and transforms the design itself.

Garutti

There's a subtle difference between this sense of engagement and the idea of participatory design.

Bolchover

We've never believed in this sort of participation through design. We come in with a degree of expertise as spatial enablers or choreographers of different actors and maintain that we have something to offer as designers. We test different methods of engagement—again, depending on the context—and scope out our control over the design. So, for instance, we're going door to door working with a group of four families in Mongolia, figuring out what their needs are and how they can imagine their sites and plots evolving. But we're not asking them to design. I don't personally believe in that kind of participation as a process.

Garutti

"Choreography" is a good word for it.

Scheinman

You've pointed out to us in the past that you sometimes forget in choreographing these relationships and having conversations with families that you actually do, in the end, make buildings. Sometimes you seem to play more of a mediating, facilitating role, with the buildings almost secondary to the relationships and networks you build on site. Sometimes, as with the As Found Houses project, you don't seem to intend to build at all. So how do the buildings come about? If it's not participatory in this sense—

Bolchover
Well, what do you mean by participatory? It seems useful to unpick what these words mean and not take them for granted.

Lin
It's important for us to retain the expertise of design, the authorship of design, and to not pretend that other people have designed it. It's about limiting our designs to a few essential things. We try to design projects so that the community can really take it over, transform it, and change it. We try not to over-program and to accept that things could evolve.

Bolchover
We had two lessons of this. One was when were in China, working on a school in Jiangxi, and the group that we were working with, the NGO, asked the children to draw their ideal school. They could draw whatever they wanted on paper, with only their imaginations, their creativity, and come up with whatever they thought their ideal schools would be. Thirty kids drew a generic, floor-slabbed school with a Chinese flag on top.

The other example is from Mongolia. We were trying to engage the community and asked them what their dreams were for these neighborhoods. And everyone just wrote "make the road better." And for me, I noticed that part of our role is to be outsiders. It's an advantageous position to come in from the outside and offer things that people would never have thought of before because they're so contained within their own contexts. They only know what they see and what they're familiar with. Part of our role as experts with our architectural mindsets is to come in and suggest something else.

The Children

7. LOCAL AND GLOBAL PRACTICE

Lin

This is another way to interpret the local and the global. Maybe it's important to be both an insider and an outsider, as Josh is saying. You look at all these things locally, but you look at it having seen other places around the world and able to see the connections between them. Sometimes that's our responsibility: to look at Mongolia and what's happening there, but with an awareness of what's happening in Latin America; to understand why it's different and ask what solutions can be transferred, what solutions are irrelevant.

Scheinman

So these same considerations, in some sense, apply universally, across the planet? I'm thinking specifically of your comparisons of the ger district in Ulaanbaatar to Paraisopolis, Brazil and Baishizhou, Shenzhen, but also of the particular uniqueness of rural Chinese development.

Bolchover

I remember a conference from when I was in London; it was called *Strangely Familiar*, and its name stuck with me. Somehow, we like to work with things that are familiar and normative but also quite other, quite strange, quite confrontational to their place or context. I think there's something about the architecture in these places that has that kind of quality. It's not completely of its place nor is it completely alien. It's hybrid; it has duality.

Lin

Our participation in these places is an attempt to allow for these places to evolve naturally. It touches on this question of architecture without architects again. When the world changes very slowly, you don't need designers, because communities can innovate according to their own needs and build for themselves. It's an inherent part of our relationship with our environment and an inherent part of how communities work. Traditional communities are always innovating, but that innovation happens over a very long period of time.

Now, as the world moves faster and faster, we witness many local places getting more and more fragmented. What we try to do in our work is that we try to create a new spatial cohesion. We try to stitch together aspects that have been fragmented by the forces acting on these areas. And we also try to create a cohesion between the past and future, between an abandonment of one way of building and the wholesale adoption of a completely new way of building. The communities we work with are interesting because they still have one foot in a certain cultural condition—they still hang onto the richness of these places—but they also want to catch up. They want to speed up toward what they perceive as a modern condition.

There's immense potential in working with these communities specifically because they present new possibilities for how development can occur. We're interested in how architecture works in dialogue with what's around it. And so the combination of alien and familiar in building becomes a vehicle for an evolution of place that remains in harmony while adapting to rapidly transforming lifestyles.

8. PLANETARY URBANIZATION
AND THE VERNACULAR

Scheiman

You earlier alluded to the idea that "vernacular" as a term is out-dated or not significant anymore. What would it be now? If vernacular today really means a romanticized look to the past, and its opposite is a universalist, concrete-tower kind of thing, what does it mean it that the Chinese villagers you're working with, for instance, want for concrete?

Bolchover

What I think is fascinating about the vernacular is that it's so different from those concrete towers. In Mongolia, with the gers, the vernacular has to be challenged. The ger is a thousands-of-years-old, perfected, nomadic structure, but it's completely useless in an urban situation. In fact, it's more than useless: it's actually the reason why the ger districts have grown so unsustainably. It's been a damaging instrument in the process of urbanization. That contradiction is fascinating to me. In the Chinese context, which is almost the opposite, maybe it's easier to look at these vernacular structures as overlooked and obsolescent but as having some underappreciated worth or value. It's about looking at something to then evolve or find the missing bridge between an existing vernacular and generic structure. In the same way, we work with the ger and the plug-in as something halfway between vernacular and urbanized. We're at that interface between an existing condition and a generic understanding of what a house is or what living is or what a dwelling is, working to reinterpret that divide to suggest a new way forward for how a context and community can evolve. Through that role, we begin to see that our operations are by necessity incremental. This idea of incremental change is part and parcel of our approach to thinking about context and how it's by definition dynamic.

Garutti

When I was with you in both China and Mongolia, the notion of vernacular seemed less like something authentic or true to tradition than like something in transformation. It was all about process.

Lin

It's great for somebody like Josh with an interest in urbanization to go and look at a culture that's fundamentally resistant to urbanization. And then to discover how a nomadic way of living enabled an extreme form of urbanization in the ger district.

Bolchover

As with most of our projects, we come across these things by chance. We're very opportunistic in a way. When we see something as an opportunity, we grab hold of it. In China, we were looking at the urbanization of the rural; in Mongolia, it's the opposite condition, where rural nomads are moving into the city. What fascinates me is what it means to *become urban*. What does it mean when your everyday life becomes fundamentally altered? What does it mean to live amongst strangers; to buy coal for fuel; to have to collect water from a kiosk rather than a stream? You have a neighbour—you've never had a neighbour before. Your degree of public life has shifted. All of these things are fundamentally transformed in this new context. And to then see how that group of people would evolve, for me, raises the fundamental questions of what it means to make a city.

What's also fascinating is the impact of architecture at a territorial scale. It's not just a matter of thinking about architecture as a singular unit, but about making links between the role of architecture and the role of urbanization. Could we actually bring these two things together? Can architecture have a role in that urbanization process? That's what the Mongolian context offers as a challenge. Not that we've achieved it yet—I think that's the ongoing project—but the ambition is to begin to synthesize a new way of thinking about the urbanization process through something as small as a dwelling unit. The ger itself produced a certain form of urbanization or urban fabric through its architecture.

Lin

Do you think we can learn from this in other cities?

Bolchover

Definitely.

Lin

It's a place where so many things are the opposite of how we see it elsewhere, how the world is today. It lends a kind of hopeful possibility. You were asking about what we can learn, and I think there's a lot to be inspired by in the innovation regular people have in building their own houses. The homes are alternative models of contemporary urban life.

Bolchover

What's also fascinating for me in Mongolia is that it acts as this kind of critical reflection. It becomes a reflective practice. It's not that we built these hybrid structures in Mongolia and now we can use them in South America. It's not that at all. It's about asking what it means to live this way and using these projects to reflect on our positions as architects and the types of urban spaces we're making. When I'm working at a site with a toxic water supply, I start thinking about our relationship to waste. So many of the things that are underlying our urban world are exposed and made transparent in this condition, and so the context here becomes a useful instrument to review how we live and how we make urban spaces anywhere.

Lin

It's a critique on how we urbanize and on conventional ideas about ownership, governance, society, and the role of the architect. If you go to the ger district, it looks like a slum because all the fences are made of refuse, sometimes with leftover planks or tree bark. But then later you find out why: it's because the government has a policy by which citizens can claim a 700-square-meter parcel of land for their own use. In order to keep track of whose parcel is whose, the government requires that owners build fences as the first thing they do when they arrive from the outskirts. And of course, the new settlers just scavenge whatever they can find because they had to in order to register this piece of land. It may look like a slum, but it's essentially a suburb. We uncover many contradictions in the places we work.

Bolchover

They're often places where that one economic or neoliberal model's forms of urbanization cannot successfully take root. Top-down planning of the ger districts is not working. It's failing. It's not been possible because of a multitude of factors, including the difficulty persuading ger district residents to exchange their land for apartments; the financial reliance on the private sector to deliver implementation; and the economic situation of the nation itself.

So yes, we like to operate in those places where the formal mechanisms of planning or of urban planning are not really possible. Or haven't been able to take root in the way they've taken root in other situations.

Lin

In that sense, places like these are useful as lenses through which to reflect on our cities, and on our lives in cities, which are increasingly conceived through a singular model of development. That's why we're so fascinated with these peripheral areas. They're not exotic in the sense of location and culture; they're on the periphery of a standard developmental model. They may initially be deemed "failures," yet they hold great potential for how we can test alternative modes of development. In order to work in these places, we have to adopt very specific and alternative working methods. So in a sense, we are also exploring the boundaries of what it means to be an architect today.

How can we engineer spaces to promote and facilitate new social relationships?

Offering common ground by building new notions of civic space

Interrupting patterns by providing possibilities for collective improvisation

A model of Skanderbeg Square and its neighbouring institutions hosts discussions on public and private space

OFFERING COMMON GROUND
Skanderbeg Square; Tirana, Albania; 2008–2017 (51N4E)

During the development of Skanderbeg Square, various major institutions facing the square reached a consensus—through extensive negotiation around a working model—as to how each would refit their respective entrances to make for a flexible and approachable public space.

The front steps of a bookshop abut the square as part of
51N4E's plan to refit the area's relationship between public
and private

The Pavement

A local bank's property, marked by textured grey pavement, meets publicly owned space in a subtle connection of private and public

Designed by 51N4E, a summer pavilion in front of a hotel invites the public to occupy privately owned space

The Ger Innovation Hub sits among many gers, or nomadic structures, in the ger district of Ulaanbaatar

OFFERING COMMON GROUND
Ger Innovation Hub; Ulaanbaatar, Mongolia; 2018–2020 (RUF)

With little prior experience of living continuously among neighbours, the formerly nomadic residents of the ger districts of Ulaanbaatar require novel forms of community infrastructure. The Ger Innovation Hub is designed as a layered structure that reinterprets the material system of the movable ger structure to address social and environmental issues in the district.

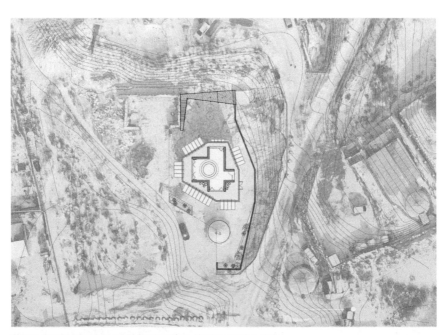

Centred on its own internal ger structure, the Innovation Hub
mirrors its surroundings in plan view

The ger form acts as a backdrop to a range of community activities

Pedestrians navigate around and through flowing water

INTERRUPTING PATTERNS
Skanderbeg Square; Tirana, Albania; 2008–2017 (51N4E)

Remotely activated through an underground technical room, a series of pumps supplies water to more than 100 outlets across the square, animating and destabilizing the unscripted life of the plaza.

Manually operated pumps feed the square's fountains

A complex set of manuals guide the workings
of the underground technical room

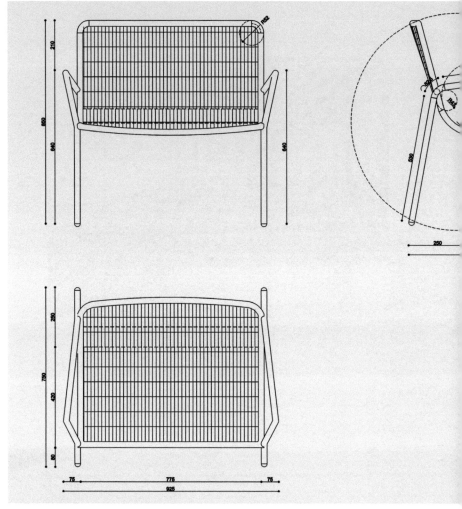

The square's love seats are designed to be both mobile and spacious

INTERRUPTING PATTERNS
Skanderbeg Square; Tirana, Albania; 2008–2017 (51N4E)

Atypically wide chairs—too big for one person but too small for two—prompt negotiation between sitters, creating moments of intimacy and making way for the informal appropriation of space. That the furniture is not fixed to the ground engages community trust.

Key infrastructure for the social life of the square,
the chairs act as instruments of improvisation

The Friends

The Shelter

How can we foster sense of place within the constraints of continual and ongoing political and cultural shifts?

Reimagining institutions to communicate transparency, openness, and the extraordinary

The Atmosphere

Created by Chevalier Masson, the centre's curtains divide a space not originally meant to be open for public use

REIMAGINING INSTITUTIONS
Centre for Openness and Dialogue; Tirana, Albania; 2015 (51N4E)

Installed under the government of Albanian prime minister Edi Rama, an illuminated sculpture at the entrance to the prime minister's office announces a new status and identity for a building previously closed to the public. In the part of the building's ground floor that is now a dedicated cultural space—including an archive, library, and exhibition hall—curtains set an intimate tone foreign to government offices, making the ambivalent space both grand and domestic.

A table, designed by 51N4E, generates differing
conditions for dialogue among meeting attendees

The Capital

The artwork *Marquee*, by Philippe Parreno, draws attention to the new entrance of what was once a private and secluded building, now beckoning the public to come inside

Part of 51N4E's plan for the building restoration, the open
ceiling represents the peeling back of a layer of architectural
program and makes space for flexibility

The sculptures were shaped by a mould of the sidewalk
so that they sit neatly in the street surface

REIMAGINING INSTITUTIONS
Bronze Monument; Tirana, Albania; 2013 (51N4E)

Four bronze sculptures along the Bulevardi Dëshmorët e Kombit (Bou-
levard of the Martyrs of the Nation) quietly mark the spots on the
pavement where four victims died during a political protest in 2011 as
perpetual shadows of a grave political history.

The hospital's continuous ramp leaves its ground floor open at the street level

REIMAGINING INSTITUTIONS
Angdong Health Centre; Baojing, Hunan, China; 2011–2016 (RUF)

Reconceived as a completely open and public institution, the Angdong Health Centre facilitates social care beyond the basic functions of a hospital. Its continuous ramp provides access to all floors of the healthcare clinic and surrounds an inner courtyard open to community use.

The Caretakers

Villagers enter the building without entering the hospital rooms, using it as a community space

REIMAGINING INSTITUTIONS
Lab North, World Trade Center I; Brussels, Belgium; 2016 (51N4E)

After decades of vacancy and disinvestment in the Northern Quarter of Brussels, creatives, academics, civic organizations, and property owners came together in a partnership to explore the future of the abandoned modern building of the World Trade Center. Over 50 organizations became temporary tenants, testing hybrid uses of the disused office spaces and turning the building into a 1:1 model for the transformation of the tower and for the district as a whole.

51N4E makes use of an unfinished floor as a temporary office

The Agreements

The building's temporary occupants come together
to discuss how to distribute space among them

How can we reorient practice to respond to increasingly complex, interwoven, and distributed contexts and site conditions?

Prompting dialogues between independent interests

Cultivating capacities by facilitating production with local materials and knowledge

Manoeuvring constraints to embrace modesty and leverage expertise

The design of the new housing structure emerged as a result of negotiations between RUF and the villagers

PROMPTING DIALOGUES
Jiaoxi Highway and Jiaohua Dam Relocations; Liuyang, Hunan, China; 2018 (RUF)

As the Chinese countryside rapidly urbanizes, villagers are incentivized to abandon their agrarian land for the development of highways and dams. Commissioned by the government to replace the abandoned village property, RUF distributed questionnaires to gauge homeowners' needs and ambitions, and to inform a model for cooperative development. Ultimately, the community dismissed all design proposals that offered new building typologies, instead readily applying their government compensation funds toward generic construction.

At a meeting to discuss relocation, government officials wait for local citizens, who would never show up

Villagers examine the model of a building proposed by RUF
before deciding against the design

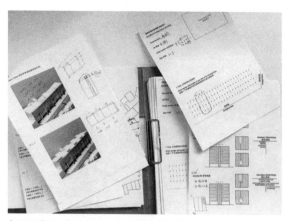

A questionnaire was used to assess villagers' needs

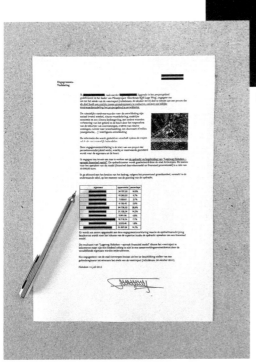

Stakeholders take in the site on "safari"

A questionnaire was used to gauge stakeholders' needs

PROMPTING DIALOGUES
Lage Weg; Antwerp, Belgium; 2015 (51N4E)

Antwerp's city and municipal governments and waste and remediation agencies commissioned a pilot project to redevelop the mixed-use site of Lage Weg. To bring together the stakeholders and establish an understanding of their ambitions for the area, 51N4E led a "site safari" to break from the typical bird's-eye presentation of masterplans.

Students and villagers install a variety of paver types

CULTIVATING CAPACITIES
Taiping Bridge; Ziyun, Guizhou, China; 2007–2009 (RUF)

In absence of the necessary funding and expertise to repair an historic bridge with traditional techniques, RUF adopted a simplified mould and cast strategy that would facilitate the combination of different modules to alternately become walking surface, planters, and seating. Over a two-week period, students and villagers worked together to install the pavers in a collaborative process that gave locals ownership of the project.

A villager removes piping from a moulded paver

Screens blocks are assembled and tested at the University of Hong Kong

The Moulds

CULTIVATING CAPACITIES
Angdong Health Centre; Baojing, Hunan, China; 2011–2016 (RUF)

Variations of a screen block for the hospital courtyard were proto-
typed at the University of Hong Kong and then sent to Baojing to be
mass produced locally. The dyed concrete blocks filter light to create soft interior spaces, while the exterior façade, constructed with
reclaimed gray bricks, give the building a quality of familiarity to the
community.

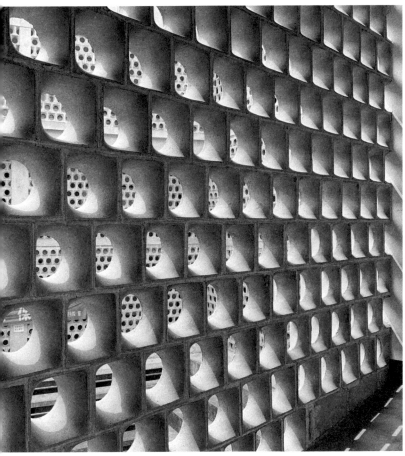

Varying orifice positions in the blocks make for distinct lighting conditions inside the hospital

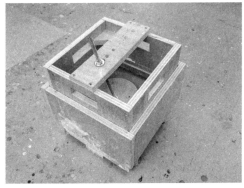

A wooden mould is used onsite for production and as a tool for engagement with local contractors

Unfinished buildings dot Tirana's outskirts

MANOEUVRING CONSTRAINTS
TID Tower; Tirana, Albania; 2004–2016 (51N4E)

To verify the TID Tower's structural feasibility and test its low-tech construction system, 51N4E erected a 1:1 partial model. Seeing the mockup together united both client and designer in a common reality. In a city characterized by unfinished buildings, the model became a part of the landscape as testimony to ongoing processes of redevelopment.

A partial model of the tower sits on the outskirts of the city

The Ground

The façade of the building in the city mirrors its 1:1 reproduction

How does a degree of unfamiliarity with the site's time and place extend design to new dimensions?

Evolving heritage to adapt custom and convention for future viability

Revitalizing ecologies by rooting urban metabolisms in local landscape and geology

The Dwellings

Designed by RUF, the tulou plug-in turns a window into a primary entrance

EVOLVING HERITAGE
Lantian Tulou; Longyan, Fujian, China; 2019 (RUF)

Constructed primarily between the twelfth and twentieth centuries, *tulous* are dwellings with thick defensive walls and large communal courtyards that reflect the organization of clans within a village. While select tulous are protected as a World Heritage Site, most are falling into disrepair and are being modified for contemporary amenities. The plug-in is one of a series of strategies to rethink the tulou through delicate intervention for contemporary ways of living together.

The plug-in is part of an overall strategy
for the tulou typology, meant to be tailored
individually to sites across the region

Since tulous are protected by heritage conventions, the plug-in design
reinvents circulation without modifying the ancient architectural form

The plug-in functions as a small library

Set back from neighbouring buildings, the walls of the new structure make for an antechamber in the space between

EVOLVING HERITAGE
BUDA Art Factory; Kortrijk, Belgium; 2005–2012 (51N4E)

With no particular spatial features demanding preservation, a former textile factory was renovated into a contemporary art space through an open approach. The new arts centre was designed for maximum indeterminacy, with generic yet warm spaces that allow for cultural production by its broadest definition.

The History

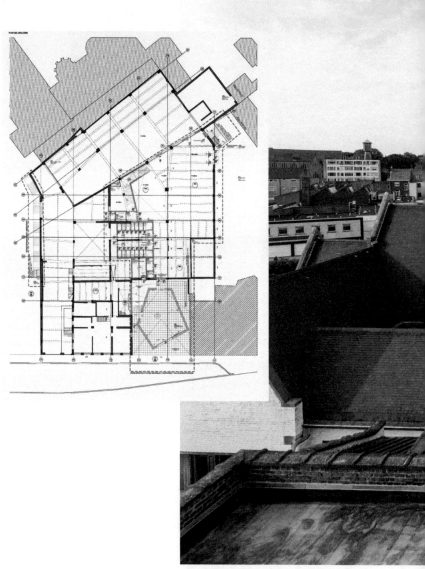

The factory both stands out and blends
in with its urban surroundings

The Quarries

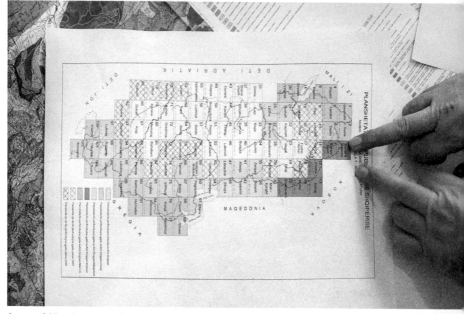

A map of Albania shows where various types of stone are found

REVITALIZING ECOLOGIES
Skanderbeg Square; Tirana, Albania; 2008–2017 (51N4E)

Sourced from Albania, the stones of Skanderbeg Square each refer to a different area of the country, acting as testimony to the region's rich resources. Together, the stones are laid out in a gradient as a mosaic of the country's geological foundations.

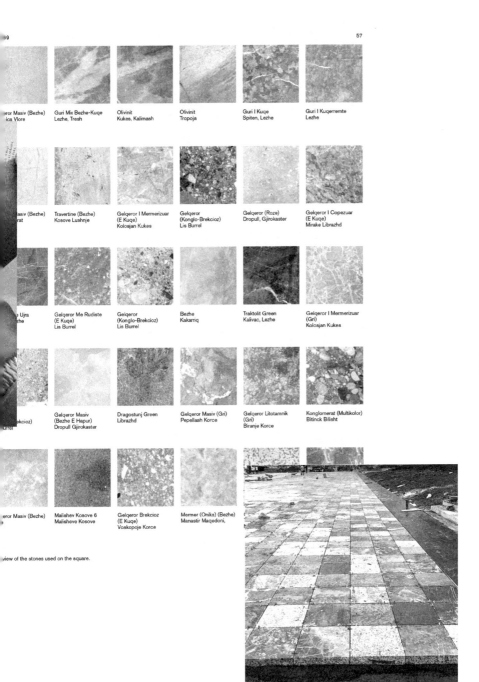

| ...ror Masiv (Bezhe) ...ica Vlore | Guri Mix Bezhe-Kuqe Lezhe, Tresh | Olivinit Kukes, Kalimash | Olivinit Tropoja | Guri I Kuqe Spiten, Lezhe | Guri I Kuqerremte Lezhe |

| ...asiv (Bezhe) ...rat | Travertine (Bezhe) Kosove Lushnje | Gelqeror I Mermerizuar (E Kuqe) Kolosjan Kukes | Gelqeror (Konglo-Brekcioz) Lis Burrel | Gelqeror (Roze) Dropull, Gjirokaster | Gelqeror I Copezuar (E Kuqe) Mirake Librazhd |

| ...e Ujra ...zhe | Gelqeror Me Rudiste (E Kuqe) Lis Burrel | Gelqeror (Konglo-Brekcioz) Lis Burrel | Bezhe Kakarriq | Traktolit Green Kalivac, Lezhe | Gelqeror I Mermerizuar (Gri) Kolosjan Kukes |

| ...ekcioz) ...rrel | Gelqeror Masiv (Bezhe E Hapur) Dropull Gjirokaster | Dragostunj Green Librazhd | Gelqeror Masiv (Gri) Pepellash Korce | Gelqeror Litotarnik (Gri) Biranje Korce | Konglomerat (Multikolor) Bitinck Bilisht |

| ...eror Masiv (Bezhe) | Malishev Kosove 6 Malisheve Kosove | Gelqeror Brekcioz (E Kuqe) Voskopoje Korce | Mermer (Oniks) (Bezhe) Manastir Maqedoni, | | |

...iew of the stones used on the square.

The square's surface acts as a material representation of the country's variation

Img. 31-32   Img. 33   34

Plant importations for the project. The plants that are originally native to Albania were no longer grown in the country and could not be sourced in local nurseries. They had to be imported from France, Belgium, Germany, and Italy as part of what was then the biggest order of perennials from Europe. Those plants thus came home, in a way, and their beauty will be revealed again to Albanians and to all the future users of the square.

Eco-regions of Albania. Albania possesses a wealth of ecosystems since it combines a very diverse geomorphology with no less than four climatic regions.

REVITALIZING ECOLOGIES
Skanderbeg Square; Tirana, Albania; 2008–2017 (51N4E)

For the green belt around the square, plants native to Albania but no longer available in the region had to be imported from France, Belgium, Germany, and Italy as part of what was then the largest order of perennials from Europe. To establish the area's ecosystem, some adult trees were planted immediately, while others live in a nursery for future integration.

The Nurseries

Published in 51N4E's book *How Things Meet*, a catalogue shows the range of plants native to Albania

Villagers use the bridge as a community space

REVITALIZING ECOLOGIES
Taiping Bridge; Ziyun, Guizhou, China; 2007–2009 (RUF)

Villagers participated in the bridge's landscaping, sourcing native plants from the neighbouring hillside and, in doing so, regenerating the site's identity.

How can we mediate among the economic and geopolitical pressures that shape our territories and cities?

Calibrating connections to the rhythms of daily life instead of the pulse of development

Anchoring growth to extend the public realm through integrated infrastructure

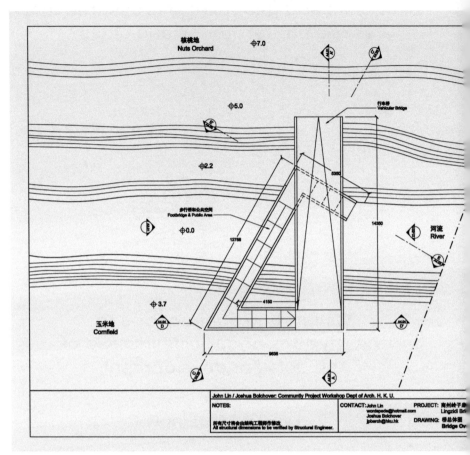

核桃地
Nuts Orchard
⊕7.0

⊕5.0

⊕2.2

行车桥
Vehicular Bridge

步行桥和公共空间
Footbridge & Public Area
⊕0.0

12788

5350

14360

河流
River

⊕3.7

玉米地
Cornfield

4150

9836

John Lin / Joshua Bolchover: Community Project Workshop Dept of Arch. H. K. U.

NOTES:

所有尺寸将会由结构工程师作修改
All structural dimensions to be verified by Structural Engineer.

CONTACT: John Lin
wordspede@hotmail.com
Joshua Bolchover
jpborch@hku.hk

PROJECT: 商州岭子桥
Lingzidi Bri

DRAWING: 桥总体图
Bridge Ov

A plan shows the difference in scale between the pedestrian bridge and railway

CALIBRATING CONNECTIONS
Lingzidi Bridge; Shangzhou, Shaanxi, China; 2011–2012 (RUF)

As China invests in large-scale infrastructure and urban development, rural communities' local networks are upended. For the construction of a new expressway, hundreds of local bridges were demolished. RUF's modest architectural intervention allows access to fields and to the river, reestablishing a link crucial to the village's economy and social fabric.

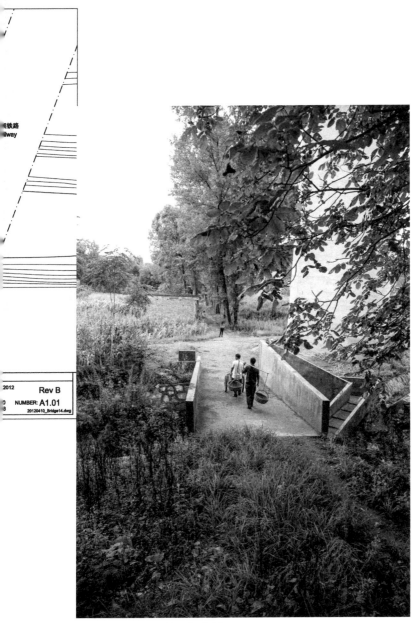

铁路
ilway

2012 Rev B
NUMBER: A1.01
20120410_Bridge14.dwg

Villagers use the pedestrian bridge

The team surveys the space
beneath the railway

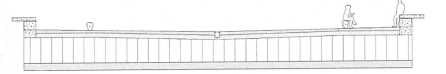

The width of the balustrade makes way for sitters,
amblers, and booksellers

CALIBRATING CONNECTIONS
Lana Bridge; Tirana, Albania; 2008 (51N4E)

A bridge already under construction on site left a very small margin of freedom for new design. The intervention by 51N4E tweaks the bridge's shape to create a convex platform, giving users an opportunity to stop for a moment by the river. An extra-wide balustrade creates an unexpected space—to be claimed, for instance, by booksellers.

More than just a path for crossing to the other side, the bridge acts
like a plaza, where pedestrians can stop and take in the city

The City

The Node

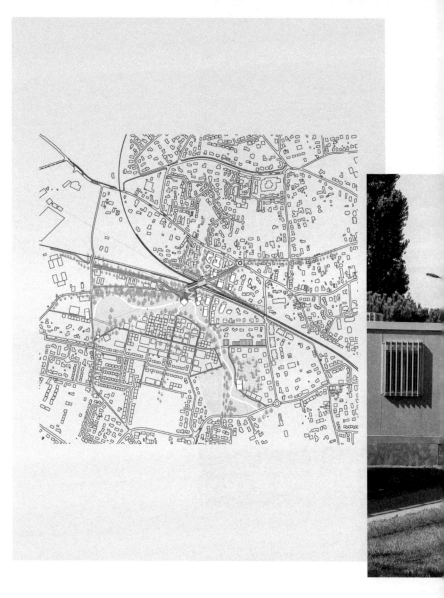

ANCHORING GROWTH
50,000 Logements; Bordeaux, France; 2010–2012 (51N4E)

A new tram links the metropolitan centre of Bordeaux to one of its suburbs, Bruges, opening the peripheral site to transit-driven housing developments. The design strategy relocates the station to the top of a bridge—a belvedere over the surrounding territory—thereby driving the prioritization of pedestrian and bicycle mobility.

The tram sits on top of a bridge, opening up space for other forms of transportation

Through use of the collection point, locals keep garbage from piling up in their district

ANCHORING GROWTH
Smart Collection Point; Ulaanbaatar, Mongolia; 2014–2015 (RUF)

Waste in the form of plastic bottles, glass, and cans is an unfamiliar phenomenon for nomads settling in the ger district of Ulaanbaatar, so it often accumulates in gullies or streams. To establish better individual and administrative practices in waste management, a pilot project initiates collaboration between the community and municipality. The prototype for a collection point, a critical infrastructural node, includes a recycling station under a ramp that splays out to create a public space.

Collection points are designed to sit along the nodes
of the district's social and infrastructural systems

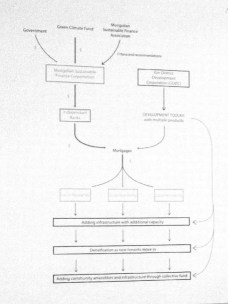

Government · Green Climate Fund · Mongolian Sustainable Finance Association

Criteria and recommendations

Mongolian Sustainable Finance Corporation

Ger District Development Corporation (GDDC)

Independent Banks

DEVELOPMENT TOOLKIT with multiple products

Mortgages

Local Residents · Local Residents · Local residents

Adding infrastructure with additional capacity

Densification as new tenants move in

Adding community amenities and infrastructure through collective fund

Mécanisme de la Société d'aménagement
urbain des quartiers de ger, 2018
Épreuve d'exposition
Rural Urban Framework

Le module d'extension de ger est un
produit conçu dans le cadre de la boîte
à outils d'aménagement progressif
(Incremental Development Toolkit
de RUF, qui permet de débloquer des
fonds publics et privés pour financer des
options d'habitation pour les résidents
aux revenus très disparates. La durabilité
environnementale et économique est
prévue dans ce prototype architectural
qui démontre qu'un aménagement urbain
à la fois écoénergétique et abordable est
possible.

Ger District Development Corporation
Mechanism, 2018
Exhibition print
Rural Urban Framework

The Ger Plug-in is a product designed as
part of RUF's Incremental Development
Toolkit, which aims to unlock public
and private funds to provide financing
options to residents with a range
of incomes. Environmental and
economic sustainability is prefigured
by the architectural prototype which
demonstrates the feasibility of low-energy
and low-cost development.

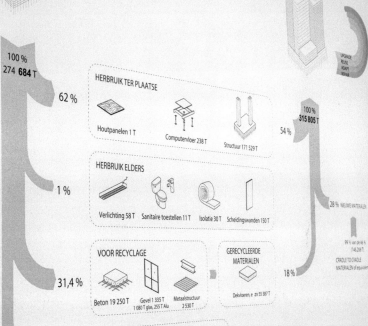

ZIN, Schéma de réutilisation, 2018
Épreuve d'exposition
51N4E, l'AUC, Jaspers-Eyers pour
Befimmo

ZIN, Schema for reuse, 2018
Exhibition print
51N4E, l'AUC, Jaspers-Eyers for
Befimmo

The construction sector produces over
628,000 tonnes of waste per year
in Brussels. Drawn up in response
the establishment of Sustainable

Usage provisoire, 2018
Épreuve d'exposition
Alexis Gicart

Suspendue entre un état de démolition
et de reconstruction, l'occupation
temporaire du bâtiment fut la
stratégie initiale permettant de tester
la plus intelligents de

Meanwhile use, 2018
Exhibition print
Alexis Gicart

With the building suspended between a
state of demolition and reconstruction,
its temporary occupation was an early
strategy to test smarter ways of working.
An intitiative by LabNorth (Up4North,
51N4E, Architecture Workroom Brussels,
Vraiment Vraiment)

14350

河流
River

...rkshop Dept of Arch. H. K. U.

CONTACT: John Lin
wordspede@hotmail.com
Joshua Bolchover
jpbarch@hku.hk

PROJECT: 商州岭子底
Lingzidi Bridge

DRAWING: ⬚⬚体
Bridge Overview

中国国家高速公路网

S/N41
Lana Bridge, 2008
Tirana, Albania
S/N41

REXHEP SHAHU
APOLOGJI

POLITIKE
MIT

Ararot la cronica
Escrabe le demoli
d'une infrastructure

How can we mediate
among the constraints
of economic and
geopolitical pressures
that shape our territories
and cities?

5IN4E

5IN4E, 2004 – 2016
Tirana, Albania

43 A decade long process of
engagement with the city
of Tirana and the Albanian
territory through a series
of encounters – formal and
informal, experiments and
failures – constituted a unique
project over time. The process
is presented in the form of a
photo-novel, in the self-initiated
publication How Things Meet.

The experience of coming into
contact with a culture and
context so different from their
own is a story of embracing
otherness and unpredictability

The project of TID Tower,
suspended for more than a year
during a process of negotiation
with the administration, was
finally relaunched with a text
message – evidence of an elastic
relation with time.

'06 '07 '08   132 133 '09 '10 '11 '12 '13 '14 '15   '16

Alban Effini

Hi ! I hope everything
s ok! Behar said to
me: let's continue
the project.
10.12.06 16:11

Options   Back

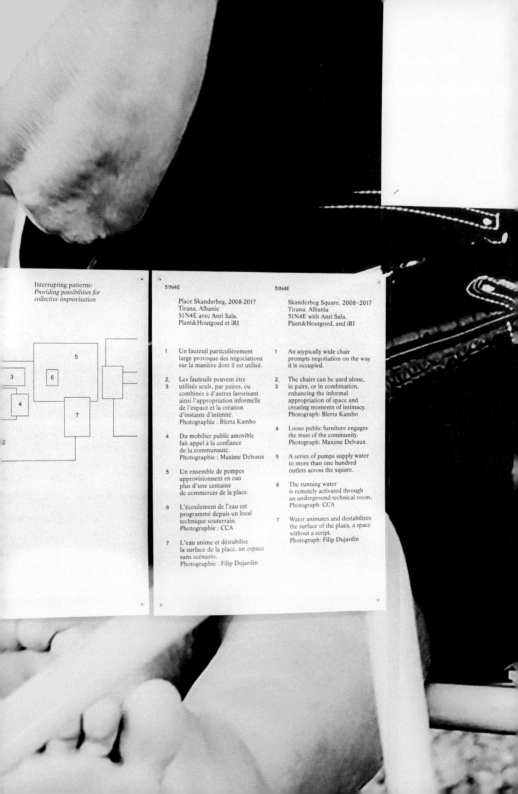

Interrupting patterns:
*Providing possibilities for
collective improvisation*

51N4E

Place Skanderbeg, 2008-2017
Tirana, Albanie
51N4E avec Anri Sala,
Plant&Houtgoed et iRI

1   Un fauteuil particulièrement
     large provoque des négociations
     sur la manière dont il est utilisé.

2,   Les fauteuils peuvent être
3   utilisés seuls, par paires, ou
     combinés à d'autres favorisant
     ainsi l'appropriation informelle
     de l'espace et la création
     d'instants d'intimité.
     Photographie : Blerta Kambo

4   Du mobilier public amovible
     fait appel à la confiance
     de la communauté.
     Photographie : Maxime Delvaux

5   Un ensemble de pompes
     approvisionnent en eau
     plus d'une centaine
     de commerces de la place.

6   L'écoulement de l'eau est
     programmé depuis un local
     technique souterrain.
     Photographie : CCA

7   L'eau anime et déstabilise
     la surface de la place, un espace
     sans scénario.
     Photographie : Filip Dujardin

51N4E

Skanderbeg Square, 2008–2017
Tirana, Albania
51N4E with Anri Sala,
Plant&Houtgoed, and iRI

1   An atypically wide chair
     prompts negotiation on the way
     it is occupied.

2,   The chairs can be used alone,
3   in pairs, or in combination,
     enhancing the informal
     appropriation of space and
     creating moments of intimacy.
     Photograph: Blerta Kambo

4   Loose public furniture engages
     the trust of the community.
     Photograph: Maxime Delvaux

5   A series of pumps supply water
     to more than one hundred
     outlets across the square.

6   The running water
     is remotely activated through
     an underground technical room.
     Photograph: CCA

7   Water animates and destabilizes
     the surface of the plaza, a space
     without a script.
     Photograph: Filip Dujardin

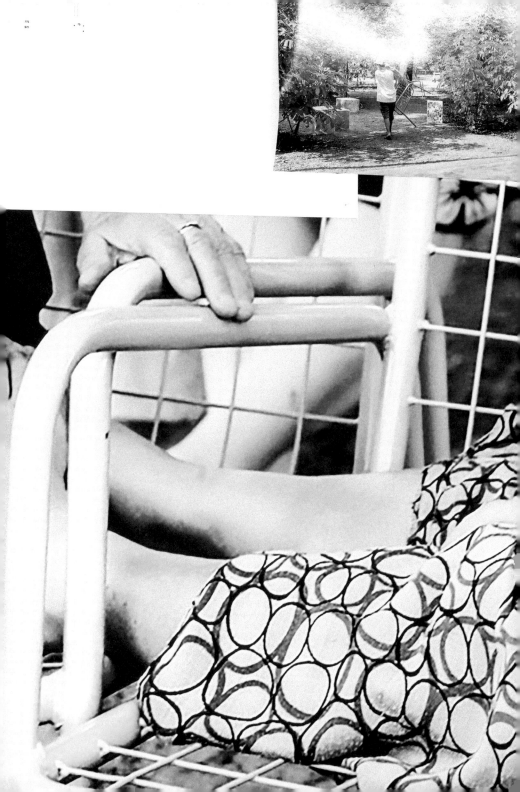

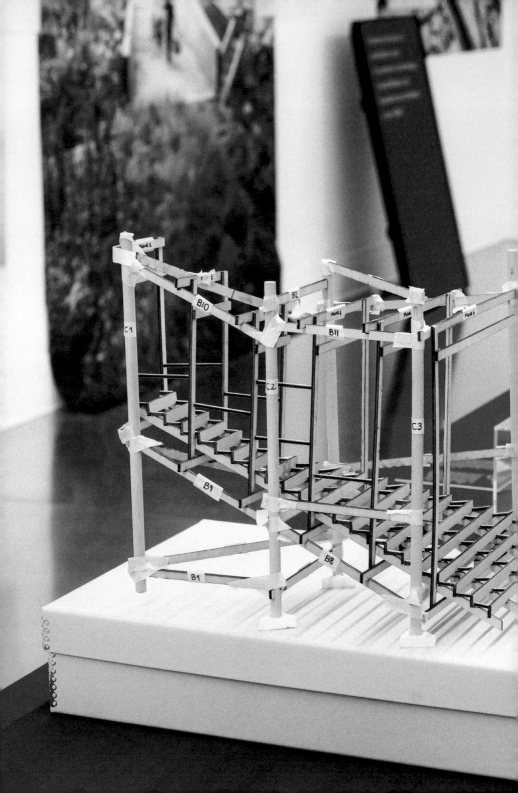

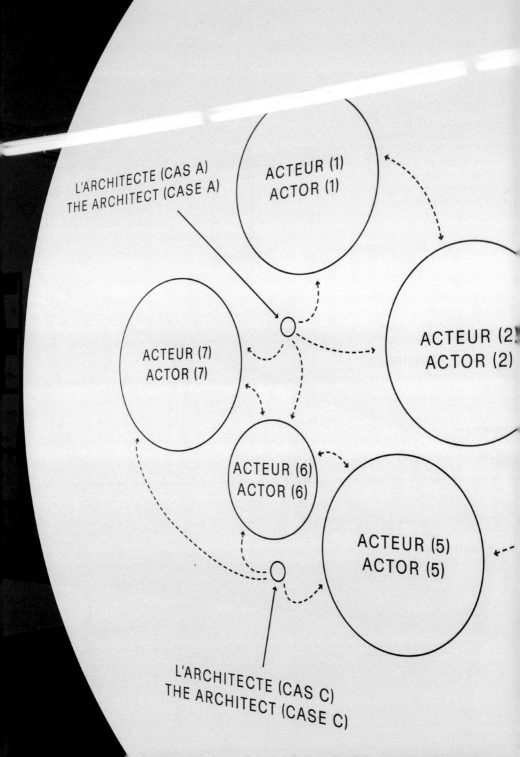

L'ARCHITECTE (CAS A)
THE ARCHITECT (CASE A)

ACTEUR (1)
ACTOR (1)

ACTEUR (2)
ACTOR (2)

ACTEUR (7)
ACTOR (7)

ACTEUR (6)
ACTOR (6)

ACTEUR (5)
ACTOR (5)

L'ARCHITECTE (CAS C)
THE ARCHITECT (CASE C)

CREDITS

COVER
The Things Around Us: 51N4E and Rural Urban Framework. Installation view, 2020 © CCA
Front cover © Rural Urban Framework
Back cover, left © Chevalier Masson; top © Rural Urban Framework; centre © CCA

STILLS FROM *Untitled (The Things Around Us)*
1, 2, 7, 10, 13, 14, 23, 34, 35, 40 © Maxime Delvaux
3 © Anji Sauvé Clubb
4 (inset) © Sertis Productions
4 (frame), 19 © 51N4E
5, 6, 8, 20, 22 (frame), 31 (frame), 33, 36, 37, 38, 41 © Rural Urban Framework
9 © Stef Hoffer/Shutterstock
11 © SvelStudio/Shutterstock
12 © TheSmurfboard
15 © CCA; *The Marquee*, 2015 © Philippe Parreno
21, 24, 25, 42 © CCA
16 © Center for Openness and Dialogue; *The Sign*, 2015 © Thomas Demand
17 China: borrowing the best of capitalism, 1984 © Associated Press
18 © Guust Selhorst
22 (inset) © Zhen Zhou
26 © Nihao Films for Fundació Mies van der Rohe
27 © RuptlyTV
28 © Karine Dana
29 © Shushodo
30 © Milosh Kitchovitch
31 (inset) © Mongol Micron Cashmere
32 © Vpro Broadcast International
39 © Devir Produções

FROM WITHIN AN ECOLOGY OF PRACTICE
44–58 © CCA

INVENTORY OF TOOLS AND TACTICS FOR TRANSFORMING CONTEXTS
106, 114, 124 (left), 130, 135, 148, 150, 151, 159, 160, 162, 163 © 51N4E
107, 108, 109, 111, 112, 113, 120, 121, 122, 124 (right), 132, 134 (top), 139 (top), 141, 142, 144, 145, 146, 165, 166 © CCA
110, 125, 126, 127, 133, 134 (bottom), 136, 137, 138, 139 (bottom), 154, 156, 157, 158, 164 © Rural Urban Framework
115, 116 © Blerta Kambo
118 © Maxime Delvaux
123, 140 © Stefano Graziani
128, 129, 147, 149 © Filip Dujardin
152, 153 © Plant en Houtgoed

SEPTEMBER 2020, MONTRÉAL
169–230 *The Things Around Us: 51N4E and Rural Urban Framework*. Installation views, 2020 © CCA

EDITOR Francesco Garutti
EDITOR-IN-CHARGE Andrew Scheinman
GRAPHIC DESIGN NLF Team, Berlin/Hamburg
RESEARCH AND EDITORIAL ASSISTANCE Irene Chin, Jann Wiegand
CCA PHOTOGRAPHY Matthieu Brouillard
RIGHTS AND REPRODUCTIONS Stéphane Aleixandre
PRODUCTION MANAGEMENT Natasha Leeman
LITHOGRAPHY Heiko Neumeister
PRINTING AND BINDING DZA Druckerei zu Altenburg

This volume is published by the Canadian Centre for Architecture (CCA) and jovis Verlag GmbH in conjunction with the exhibition *The Things Around Us: 51N4E and Rural Urban Framework*, organized by and presented at the CCA from 16 September 2020 to 19 September 2021.

CURATOR Francesco Garutti
CONCEPT Johan Anrys, Joshua Bolchover, John Lin, Freek Persyn
CURATORIAL COORDINATION Irene Chin
EXHIBITION DESIGN 51N4E (Freek Persyn with Roxane Le Grelle and Sébastien Roy), Brussels; Rural Urban Framework (Joshua Bolchover and John Lin with Chiara Oggioni), Hong Kong
DESIGN DEVELOPMENT Sébastien Larivière, Jasmine Graham
GRAPHIC DESIGN Something Fantastic, Berlin

The CCA is an international research centre and museum founded by Phyllis Lambert in 1979 on the conviction that architecture is a public concern. Through its collection, exhibitions, public programs, publications, and research opportunities the CCA advances knowledge, promotes public understanding, and widens thought and debate on architecture, its history, theory, practice, and its role in society today.

The Things Around Us: 51N4E and Rural Urban Framework is part of a CCA series that pairs distinctive architectural cases in order to investigate and interrogate current ideas in thinking and practice. In developing an installation within the context of the CCA galleries and partic-ipating in the accompanying publication, participating architects are given the opportunity to contribute to and shape a larger conversation on concepts with particular relevance for the CCA. Previous projects in the series include *Besides History: Go Hasegawa, Kersten Geers, David Van Severen* (CCA, Koenig Books, and Kajima Institute Publishing, 2018), *Rooms You May Have Missed: Umberto Riva, Bijoy Jain* (CCA and Lars Müller Publishers, 2015), *Other Space Odysseys: Greg Lynn, Michael Maltzan, Alessandro Poli* (CCA and Lars Müller Publishers, 2010), *Some Ideas on Living in London and Tokyo by Stephen Taylor and Ryue Nishizawa* (CCA and Lars Müller Publishers, 2008), and *Environment: Approaches for Tomorrow – Gilles Clément, Philippe Rahm* (CCA and Skira, 2006).

The CCA gratefully acknowledges the support of the ministère de la Culture et des Communi-cations du Québec, the Canada Council for the Arts, and the Conseil des arts de Montréal.